GW01072012

THEY HAVE FORGOTTEN...

An urgent plea for evangelicals to recognise the danger of the Ecumenical Movement and remember the stand that the British Evangelical Council and Dr. Martyn Lloyd-Jones took against it.

R. E. PALGRAVE

UNITY IN TRUTH LITERATURE

They Have Forgotten...

An urgent plea for evangelicals to recognise the danger of the Ecumenical Movement and remember the stand that the British Evangelical Council and Dr. Martyn Lloyd-Jones took against it.

ISBN 978-0-9572578-0-1

Published by Unity in Truth Literature
P.O. Box 4357, CARDIFF, CF14 8HY, Wales, UK.

For further copies of this booklet
E-mail: unityintruth@hotmail.co.uk
Telephone: 07967 118852

All Scripture quotations are from the Authorised (King James) Version unless otherwise stated.

Front cover photograph by Ed Freeman of Ruby Beach, Olympic Peninsula, Washington, USA. Used by permission of Getty Images.

Printed by Spectrum Printing, Cardiff, UK.

Contents

Foreword by Rev. Harry Waite*

It is a high honour to write a foreword to this vital document. The progress of compromise and fundamental error has spread over these Isles alarmingly for many years. The time came when a stand for truth and righteousness was essential. In the 1960s the World Council of Churches was gathering momentum and luring many churches into its folds. God raised up a faithful and brilliant man of God, Dr. Martyn Lloyd-Jones, His gift to a seriously drifting church in the land. He took a stand for Biblical truth and the necessity for separation from apostasy. The BEC was led by a faithful General Secretary, Rev. Hon. Roland Lamb. Many ministers joined this noble stand for the Word of God.

In the process of time, alas, the situation rapidly deteriorated and deadly darkness has overreached the churches. Many evangelicals have forgotten the stand of Dr. Lloyd-Jones and the BEC against the Ecumenical Movement. Recently, a bright light shone amidst the gloom and a document has been produced with faithful accuracy of the history, detailing the facts of these brave and Biblically faithful times when the Word of God held sway.

The one and only hope for genuine Christianity is a mighty outpouring of the Holy Spirit. God only honours His Truth. This wonderful history recorded in the booklet will greatly stimulate an urgent cry to Christ to revive His churches and bring in a multitude of all ages to be born again by the Holy Spirit.

The Lord Jesus Christ said 'I will build my church; and the gates of hell shall not prevail against it' (Matt. 16:18). Oh may God in His mercy save multitudes of precious souls perishing in their sins and rushing into perdition; all for the glory of God.

---

* Rev. Harry Waite was a member of the Westminster Fellowship when it was chaired by Dr. Lloyd-Jones. (The Westminster Fellowship began in 1941 as a meeting at Westminster Chapel for pastors and men in positions of Christian leadership). Rev. Harry Waite was the pastor of Thornton Heath Evangelical Church from 1959 to 1993 and is currently the pastor of Carmel Evangelical Church in Christchurch, near Bournemouth.

Introduction

The British Evangelical Council (BEC) was formed in 1952 in response to the threat posed to the Gospel by the World Council of Churches (WCC) and the Ecumenical Movement. Rev. E. J. Poole-Connor[1] was the BEC's first leader and he made a strong and faithful stand, producing helpful literature in order to warn Christians of the dangers of joining with Rome and the WCC.

In 1967 the Rev. Hon. Roland Lamb became the General Secretary of the BEC, serving in this role until 1982. He understood that the defence of the Faith was costly, having himself seceded from the Methodist denomination, deeply troubled by its departure from the fundamental truths of the Bible. In the 1960s Dr. Martyn Lloyd-Jones[2] allied himself with the BEC, and together with Rev. Roland Lamb made a valiant Biblical stand for the Gospel, against the Ecumenical Movement and for true Christian unity amongst evangelicals standing apart from this apostasy.

In 1968 the BEC issued a statement setting out its stand against the Ecumenical Movement. The Council said that it was its 'earnest hope and prayer' that the information in the document entitled *Official Statement: Attitude to Ecumenicity*

> '...would prove to be of constructive help to all evangelicals at the present time and help to prevent needless misunderstanding concerning the Council's aims and policy.'

Sadly, the stand of the BEC has been largely forgotten. There has also been much confusion regarding Dr. Lloyd-Jones' views on separation from error and the exact stand that he took, especially in regard to evangelicals in the mixed denominations. Furthermore, in 2004 the name of the BEC was changed to *Affinity* and significant changes have occurred in the organisation.

As Dr. Lloyd-Jones warned:

> '"All institutions tend to produce their opposite"... [this] has become true of [the] denominations... So there is this testimony from history to the terrible danger of institutions which start on the right lines and excellently, gradually changing, almost imperceptibly, into something which is almost the exact opposite. That fact in and of itself is sufficient cause to examine ourselves on this occasion.'[3]

There is therefore a desperate need today to re-examine the faithful stand that Dr. Lloyd-Jones and the BEC took against the Ecumenical Movement and the reason that the stand was so necessary in both their day and in ours. For this reason, this booklet will quote heavily from the sermons and addresses of Dr. Lloyd-Jones and the BEC's *Official Statement: Attitude to Ecumenicity*.

1. Dr. Lloyd-Jones' plea for evangelicals to take a definite stand against the World Council of Churches

Dr. Lloyd-Jones saw the Ecumenical Movement as Satan's master plan of attack on the Gospel in modern times and made an urgent plea to evangelicals that:

> '...we should take a definite stand against the World Council of Churches and its teaching ...[because] we believe that the World Council and the great world church that it is hoping to form is going to be the greatest hindrance of all to the preaching of this Gospel and the salvation of the souls of men and women.'[4]

However, since the WCC came into being there has been division amongst evangelicals with regard to it. There are those who feel that obedience to God and to His Truth means that they *must* stand totally clear of what they perceive to be an unbiblical and dangerous movement; some evangelicals outside the WCC have no problem associating with churches in the WCC, and there are evangelicals remaining within the WCC itself. As Dr. Lloyd-Jones said:

> 'I stand for evangelical unity – and so does the British Evangelical Council. You will have noticed that there is a disagreement between evangelicals at the present time... there are some of us who believe that the World Council of Churches has introduced a new element into the situation which calls for a definite stand on our part. This is where this division comes, and **it has been opened up by the World Council of Churches**.
>
> ...We, in the British Evangelical Council, hold the view that not only can we do nothing to further the work of the World Council of Churches, but that we are called upon to oppose and resist it with all the might and strength and power that God gives us.'[5]

Dr. Lloyd-Jones went on to warn of the great confusion amongst unbelievers as to God's Truth that was being caused by evangelicals remaining in mixed denominations and the Ecumenical Movement. Dr. Lloyd-Jones' words are just as pertinent today:

> '... we realize that we are in the midst of a very great battle and that the greatest tragedy of the hour is the confusion of the Christian church with regard to it... – if the trumpet gives an uncertain sound, who shall prepare himself for the battle?'[6]

Sadly the confusion today is far greater than ever before amongst evangelicals as to the Biblical teaching regarding separation from error, and amongst unbelievers as to the nature of real Christianity. Furthermore, the Ecumenical Movement has grown dramatically in its power, scope and momentum and is much nearer to its goal now than ever before. Most tragically, the faithful stand of the BEC and Dr. Lloyd-Jones has been forgotten by many evangelicals. In discussions with the younger generation of Christians, it is clear that the vast majority lack an understanding of the beliefs and aims of the Roman Catholic Church and the dangers of the Ecumenical Movement, and know nothing at all of the stand of Dr. Lloyd-Jones and the BEC. Furthermore, it is apparent that younger ministers believe that the threat of the Ecumenical Movement has completely disappeared and hence see no reason to educate their people in these matters. Sadly, it can indeed be said that 'My people are destroyed for lack of knowledge' (Hosea 4:6).

As this booklet will show, the Ecumenical Movement and the threat of a World Church uniting 'Christian' and non-Christian religions has not disappeared. A Biblical stand for Truth **in order to protect the precious Gospel of our Lord and Saviour Jesus Christ** is therefore desperately required in our day. Satan has cleverly taken the eyes of evangelicals away from the WCC and its steady growth in power. Meanwhile, he is busy sewing links between evangelicals and Rome any way he can. Some of these links are direct and obvious and some less obvious but just as effective in drawing evangelicals onto his path to Rome.

The Charismatic Movement and its heavily ecumenical 'Contemporary Christian Music'[7] play a major part in today's Roman Catholic Church and in ecumenical meetings,[8] and are being embraced by evangelicals today. As Dr. Peter Masters has warned, it may well be that Satan's plan to make Rome acceptable to evangelicals is:

> '...by the standardisation of contemporary Christian worship, charismatic practice, and similar trends. After all, if he can persuade all to worship and act in the same way, all will soon 'feel' they are the same.'[9]

The Emerging Church[10] movement with its Roman Catholic rituals, mysticism and worldliness is influencing evangelicals through books, videos and websites. Perhaps most significantly the New Evangelicalism (see Chapter 2), which fails to separate from or warn against error, has opened the door to Rome for the more doctrinally sound churches. Evangelical and Reformed ministers, by mixing in Charismatic and Emerging Church circles and failing to denounce error, are creating further confusion as to the line between truth and error and are leading precious souls astray.

Before examining the stand that the BEC and Dr. Lloyd-Jones took against the Ecumenical Movement, we must first consider the New Evangelicalism, to see why faithful men are so concerned by the outlook.

2. New Evangelicalism and the path to Rome

The shift in evangelical thinking away from Biblical separation and defence of the Truth to a dislike of separation from error and of contending for the Truth has undoubtedly paved the way for unity between evangelicals and Rome.[11] Indeed, the evidence shows that from its very inception, this was precisely the aim of New Evangelicalism as evidenced in the following report by the Evangelist Monroe Parker:[12]

'...in 1945, I was doing summer school work at Princeton Theological Seminary. The late Dr. John MacKay, then president of the seminary, returned from Amsterdam where he had helped to lay the foundation for the World Council of Churches. He gathered the faculty and students of the seminary on the campus. Dr. MacKay stood on the steps of Miller Hall and spoke on the Ecumenical Movement. He said that several great denominations were coming together, that the Roman Catholics would be observing, that the Greek Catholics would join, and that the Pentecostals would likely join. "But," he said, "we are going to need the evangelicals." He also said, **"There must be a Neo-Evangelicalism."** He then delineated what the characteristics of the so-called 'Neo-Evangelicalism' must be. Dr. Ockenga,[13] in that convocation speech at Fuller Theological Seminary three years later, also delineated what this Neo-Evangelicalism must be. They were almost identical to the things Dr. MacKay had delineated and that other liberals were saying at that time.'[14]

This change of direction in Evangelicalism away from the defence of Scriptural Truth became clearer in 1948 through Harold J. Ockenga who declared that:

'The ringing call for a repudiation of separatism... received a hearty response from many evangelicals... [Neo-Evangelicalism] differed from fundamentalism in its **repudiation of separatism** and its determination to engage itself in the theological dialogue of the day. It had a new emphasis upon the application of the Gospel to the sociological, political, and economic areas of life.'[15]

In terms of doctrinal controversy, the New Evangelical prefers to state positive truth only and avoid controversy and contending for the Truth. Harold J. Ockenga announced that:

'The strategy of the New Evangelical is the positive proclamation of the truth in distinction from all errors... Instead of attack upon error, the New Evangelicals proclaim the great historic doctrines of Christianity.'[16]

The New Evangelical therefore focuses on the preaching of the Gospel but fails to warn against and separate from false doctrine and false teachers in his pulpit preaching. It is fair to say that the New Evangelical may not be unconcerned about false doctrine. Some, with good motives, have the naive and unbiblical belief that simply preaching the Gospel will be enough to refute all error. They may also have a dread of controversy and this inevitably results in a failure to be faithful and warn, and in the spread of error.

Biblically-based evangelicals are very different in their thinking. Dr. Lloyd-Jones, in his BEC address *Sound An Alarm*, warned against the New Evangelical philosophy (also prominent in New Age[17] thinking) of always being positive:

> 'There are those who are just saying nothing. These are the people who claim to be ultra-spiritual. Their claim is that they are always positive. They never denounce anything. They are much too nice for that; they are much too loving. They are always preaching a positive Gospel. They never criticise wrong teaching; they never say that they are against anything at all. They are just doing their own work and preaching a positive Gospel. What is the answer to them?
>
> Well, this is how Luther answered them: "He therefore is a faithful shepherd who not only feeds but also guards the sheep. This is done when he finds out heresies and errors."...A shepherd who does not guard and protect his sheep is in the last analysis a hireling. Shepherds not only feed, but guard and protect the flock. Never was there a greater need of such a ministry than at this present time.'[18]

In his address *The Basis of Christian Unity* Dr. Lloyd-Jones pointed to the New Testament as proof that the new attitudes entering Evangelicalism were unbiblical:

> 'Look also at the language used by Jude. Look at the language used in the letters to the churches in Revelation 2 and 3. The New Testament talks about people being carried away with "strong delusion," and as people believing "a lie" (2 Thess. 2:11). The false prophets are referred to as "dogs," as those who teach and speak "damnable heresies," whose ways are pernicious and who are "liars." It refers to false teaching as a canker, a cancer that eats away at the vitals of life. That is New Testament teaching. But all that is abominated today and is regarded as being a complete denial of the spirit of love and of fellowship, indeed of the spirit of Christ.
>
> In other words, this modern teaching about unity has departed so far from the New Testament that it dislikes any polemical element at all in the preaching and the teaching of the truth. As I say, we are told that we must never be negative, that we should always be positive. The man who is admired is the man who says, I am not a controversialist, I am simply a preacher of the gospel!'[19]

Other Biblically-based evangelicals have made this same point. As the Reformed theologian Prof. John Murray[20] once said:

> 'The evangelical must indeed preach the gospel in its integrity and purity *and* preach it in its direct bearing upon the unbelief of which the same modernists are the exponents. Otherwise he is unfaithful to his evangelical witness— preaching must be negative as well as positive.'[21]

J. Sidlow Baxter[22] once referred to the 'sickly kindness' of people who 'tolerate teachers of errors in our pulpits because they are such smooth-mannered and amiable gentlemen.'[23] Regarding the dislike of controversy so common amongst New Evangelicals today, the Scottish preacher Robert Haldane[24] once said:

> 'Many religious persons have a dread of controversy and wish truth to be stated without any reference to those who hold the opposite errors. Controversy and a bad spirit are, in their estimation, synonymous terms, and strenuously to oppose what is wrong is considered as contrary to Christian meekness. Those who hold this opinion seem to overlook what every page of the New Testament lays before us. In all the history of our Lord Jesus Christ, we never find Him out of controversy... Nor did He, with all the heavenly meekness which in Him shone so brightly, treat truth and error without reference to those who held them or study to avoid giving its proper appellation to those corruptions in doctrine or practice that endangered the interests of immortal souls...'[25]

Rev. Geoff Thomas[26] has echoed these thoughts in our day and also pointed to the experience of the Apostle Paul who preached the Gospel *and* refuted error wherever he went:

> 'We cannot be wiser or more loving than the Lord Jesus Christ can we? He warned us of the danger of false prophets, and named the Pharisees as being white-washed sepulchres, full of dead bones and nothing else. The Apostle Paul publicly named and denounced false teachers and warned a congregation if anyone preached another Gospel than the one they had heard from him to let that man be accursed. The Holy Spirit gave the Apostle those words to record, so let us not grieve the Spirit by ignoring His warning.'[27]

It is not only the fear of controversy that silences men when they should speak out against error. Men may also fear persecution or the loss of popularity or usefulness within certain circles. C. H. Spurgeon warned that:

> 'It is the devil's logic which says, "You see I cannot come out and avow the Truth of God because I have a sphere of usefulness which I hold by

temporising with what I fear may be false." O Sirs, what have we to do with consequences? Let the heavens fall but let the good man be obedient to his Master and loyal to His Truth. O man of God, be just and fear not! The consequences are with *God*— not with you!'[28]

Biblically-based evangelicals have understood from personal experience of standing for the Truth, refuting error and reproving the unfruitful works of darkness that '...*all* that will live godly in Christ Jesus shall suffer persecution' (2 Tim. 3:12). In his sermon entitled *The Christian and Persecution* Lloyd-Jones said:

'The Christian is like his Lord, and this is what our Lord said about him: "*Woe unto you, when all men shall speak well of you*! *for so did their fathers to the false prophets*" (Luke 6:26). And yet is not our idea of what we call the perfect Christian nearly always that he is a nice, popular man who never offends anybody, and is so easy to get on with?... that is not the real Christian, because the real Christian is a man who is not praised by everybody. They did not praise our Lord, and they will never praise the man who is like Him.'[29]

C. H. Spurgeon, who understood that the amiability that avoids persecution is not godliness but rather the absence of godliness and love for the souls of others, summed up the true Biblical response to error:

'I take it that no honest man ought to hold his tongue concerning any of the errors of the day— it is a dishonest way of cultivating ease for yourself and gaining a popularity not worth the having! We must speak the Truth of God whether we offend or please, but this is to be done *in* love and *because* of love. God save us from that suggestion of Satan which advises us to speak only those soft things which please men's ears, for he who gives way to this persuasion is a traitor to Truth and to the souls of men. The true man of God *must* speak against every evil and false way— but there beats in his heart a strong affection to every child of God— whatever his errors and his faults may be.

The knife of the surgeon is mercifully cruel to the cancer, not out of ill-will to his patient, but out of an honest desire to benefit him. Such affectionate faithfulness we have need to cultivate. Love to the saints is the token of the saints...'[30]

The 'repudiation of separation' that Ockenga identified as a mark of New Evangelicalism may also result in a failure to separate on a church level from false teaching, and even in communications with false teachers through denominational ties, unwisely entering into dialogue and discussion with them and ignoring the Biblical warning to 'Be not deceived: evil communications corrupt good manners' (1 Cor. 15:33). As Ernest Pickering[31] stated:

'While not all new and young evangelicals[32] find fellowship within the so-called old-line denominations, generally speaking they would defend the concept of doing so.'[33]

It can therefore be seen that in its failure to warn against false teaching and separate from it, New Evangelicalism disregards Biblical teaching such as the following:

'...he that is spiritual **judgeth all things**' (1 Cor. 2:15).

'**Prove ALL things**, hold fast that which is good' (1 Thess. 5:21).

'And have no fellowship with the unfruitful works of darkness, **but rather reprove them**' (Eph. 5:11).

'...ye should **earnestly contend for the faith**... For there are certain men crept in unawares, who were before of old ordained to this condemnation, ungodly men, turning the grace of our God into lasciviousness, and denying the only Lord God, and our Lord Jesus Christ' (Jude 3-4).

What did the BEC make of the New Evangelicalism? The BEC's early leaders were greatly concerned and warned of its dangers. Rev. David Fountain expressed the concern of Rev. E. J. Poole-Connor as follows:

'The "new evangelicalism" that had arisen was a departure from the old. It stood for "infiltration" and not "separation."'[34]

In 1971 the BEC issued the following statement in the *BEC Newsletter* warning evangelicals of the danger of New Evangelicalism:

'The new evangelicals have also moved against most forms of separatism. Rather than repudiate those in theological error they prefer to stand on equal academic footing and enter dialogue...

Now in all Christian affection, we recognise these men as being our brothers in the Lord but we are no less concerned about their views than a man is concerned when he discovers his child has swallowed rat poison. For the Lord's sake they are dear but therein there is a deadly enemy.

Neo-evangelicalism is dangerous because it is ultimately totally destructive to the integrity and authority of the Bible. It blurs considerably the unique distinctiveness of our evangelical heritage and is therefore a compromise of revealed truth. It is dangerous because it is becoming accepted, unwittingly, by many as being perfectly faithful and true evangelicalism but to their ultimate detriment...

The new evangelicalism is a mongrel theology, a hybrid, the offspring of a forbidden relationship between light and darkness. A slippery, evasive foe, with combatants unwilling to be named...'[35]

Dr. Lloyd-Jones recognised that the New Evangelicalism that infiltrated the churches in his day would lead to associations between evangelicals, the Church of England and with Rome. He commented:

'A new climate of opinion has come in very rapidly... they are utterly impatient with those who demand true doctrine... they have a hearty dislike of prophets. They want innocuous, harmless men who won't upset anyone at all. The whole climate of thinking has ceased to be evangelical... Yet evangelicals say, "Always be positive." Even with regard to Rome a new language is coming in. The Church of England is being called a "bridge church" and there is a readiness to believe that Rome is changing...'[36]

C. H. Spurgeon specifically warned about the dangers of silence in the face of ecumenical error and Rome:

'It is impossible but that the Church of Rome must spread, when we who are the watchdogs of the fold are silent, and others are gently and smoothly turfing the road, and making it as soft and smooth as possible, that converts may travel down to the nethermost hell of Popery. We want John Knox back again. Do not talk to me of mild and gentle men, of soft manners and squeamish words, we want the fiery Knox, and even though his vehemence should "ding our pulpits into blads," it were well if he did but rouse our hearts to action.'[37]

Furthermore, if Martin Luther, the great reformer who stood so valiantly against the Roman Catholic Church and her heresies, could speak to us today, his voice would ring out once again with these powerful words of condemnation in the ears of the New Evangelical:

'If I profess with the loudest voice and clearest exposition every portion of the Word of God except precisely that little point which the world and the devil are at that moment attacking, I am not confessing Christ, however boldly I may be professing Him. Where the battle rages there the loyalty of the soldier is proved; and to be steady on all the battle front besides, is mere flight and disgrace if he flinches at that point.'[38]

It is against this backdrop of New Evangelicalism that has overtaken churches today that we will now look at the Ecumenical Movement itself and then examine the precise stand of Dr. Lloyd-Jones and the BEC.

3. The Ecumenical Movement and the World Council of Churches

The Ecumenical Movement began in 1910 but became 'an urgent problem'[39] in 1948 when the World Council of Churches (WCC) was officially formed in Amsterdam. The WCC is an international ecumenical union of over 350 denominations in 120 countries. As E. J. Poole-Connor warned, the WCC's 'final goal [is] the re-establishment of One Visible Church.'[40] This is based upon a misunderstanding of the Scriptural teaching in John 17 where our blessed Lord Jesus Christ prayed for unity. Dr. Lloyd-Jones showed that the unity of John 17 is that of regenerate believers, therefore we are to *keep the unity* that we already have, and that this unity is unity *in* the Truth. As Hugh Latimer, who was burned at the stake for his confession of faith, cried out: 'Unity must be according to God's Holy Word, or else it were better war than peace.'[41]

Evangelicals saw the unscriptural basis of the WCC and the inherent danger, and in 1952 the BEC was founded. In 1968 the BEC published a policy statement regarding the Ecumenical Movement stating that the aim of the Council was to:

> '...draw together those churches which are one on the fundamental doctrines of the faith, which desire to discover and experience that true ecumenicity which the Scriptures certainly teach, and which are therefore also united in their opposition to the development of that form of unscriptural ecumenicity represented by the World Council of Churches.'[42]

The BEC warned that:

> 'By its ambiguity and permitted latitude of interpretation the doctrinal basis of the World Council of Churches, so far from being an adequate safeguard against heresy, is rather a cover for it so that within its ranks are found church bodies who hold modernist, Sacramentarian and even Unitarian views.'[43]

Since then other forms of apostasy have been evident in the WCC. For example, at the WCC conference in November 1993 the idol Sophia, the 'Biblical goddess of creation,' was honoured by feminists, a Buddhist prayed to the trees and liberals declared that man does not need atonement and described God as an 'abusive parent.' In 1984 the WCC published *No Longer Strangers,*[44] which instructed women to pray to God by the following names: Lady of Peace, Lady of Wisdom, Lady of Love, Lady of Birth, Lord of Stars, Lord of Planets, Mother, Bakerwoman, Presence, Power, Essence and Simplicity. Following the 1991 WCC conference it was reported that: 'The World Council of Churches took Ecumenism to its farthest limits… suggesting Muslims, Hindus and others achieve salvation in the same way as Christians and warning the latter against "narrow thinking."'[45]

It was reported that at the WCC's Ninth Assembly[46] in 2006, an evening interfaith peace rally was led by 'a Buddhist monk, a Muslim Imam and an Anglican bishop... Representatives of each "religious tradition" played a role in offering audible prayers to "the spirit of the universe."'[47]

The Doctrine Commission of the Church of England, a member of the WCC, has stated that '...for many Christians today the idea of God offering himself as a substitute for our sins is deeply repellent.'[48] The gross error and blasphemy of the WCC and its members is therefore undeniable.

At the massive ecumenical conference with 50,000 participants, entitled *Unity in the Lordship of Jesus,* held in Kansas City in 1977, the Catholic Charismatic Kevin Ranaghan[49] announced that the streams of Christianity were uniting. The popular Charismatic Jamie Buckingham[50] said: 'We cannot have unity based on doctrine. Doctrine will always separate the body of Christ...'[51]

In 1986 the Day of Prayer for World Peace (repeated in 1993 and 2002) was held in Assisi, Italy, led by Pope John Paul II, and included Anglicans, the Archbishop of Canterbury[52] and the Baptist World Alliance.[53] It was reported that:

> '...130 leaders of the world's 12 major religions [gathered] to pray for peace. Praying together were snake worshipers, fire worshipers, spiritists, animists, North American witch doctors, Buddhists, Muslims, and Hindus, as well as "Christians" and Catholics. The Pope declared that all were "praying to the same God." On that occasion the Pope allowed his good friend the Dalai Lama to replace the cross with Buddha on the altar of St. Peter's Church in Assisi and for him and his monks to perform their Buddhist worship there.'[54]

Although the Roman Catholic Church is not officially a member of the WCC it has, however, worked closely with the WCC since the 1960s, and today many of the leaders of the WCC are Catholics. The aim of the Roman Catholic Church is to get Protestants within its fold once more and, as Dr. Lloyd-Jones warned, it has not changed its doctrinal stance towards Protestantism but is calling us 'separated brethren' and presenting a friendly face in order to beguile us.[55] Edward Panosian[56] has said:

> 'Rome's conception of the Ecumenical Movement is the joining of all churches - eventually all religions - to Rome. Rome does not join the WCC; she invites the WCC to join her. The whole Ecumenical programme has been called "the reversal of the Reformation."'[57]

4. The attitude of Dr. Lloyd-Jones and the BEC towards the Ecumenical Movement

The BEC stated that it aimed to alert Christians to all the subtle and dangerous departures from the true evangelical faith and of the perils of the Ecumenical Movement which threatened Biblical truth.[58]

As a believer in, and defender of, the pure Gospel of God, the BEC declared that:

> '... we cannot be associated in any way with a movement which implies that the evangelical position is but one of the many insights or traditions and which necessarily requires evangelical churches, directly or indirectly associated with it, to be in fellowship as fellow-Christian churches with religious bodies which do not hold to the very essentials of Biblical Christianity. Thus to be publicly allied with liberal and sacerdotal traditions which do not recognise the complete, sufficient revelation of the Scriptures, nor the full, final and sufficient redemption that is in Christ is to compromise, if not to deny, the Gospel.'[59]

The BEC was not formed merely to stand against the apostasy in the WCC but also to promote a visible unity between true churches of Christ, and believed that 'evangelical churches ought to be seen to be in fellowship with each other and not with those who reject the authority of Scripture and the complete work of Christ.'[60]

For this reason, Dr. Lloyd-Jones dissociated himself from the Evangelical Alliance[61] and publicly allied himself with the BEC and its attitude towards the Ecumenical Movement:

> 'The Evangelical Alliance had functioned as a kind of co-ordinating body, keeping evangelical people together on a common basis, but it decided to adopt a position to the World Council of Churches which it described as "benevolent neutrality." To me that was the real turning-point. I felt that I could no longer belong to that body nor function in connection with it. It was, of course, an anomalous position for the Evangelical Alliance to take because it has, almost from the beginning, been governed by Anglican evangelicals and the Church of England was already a constituent member of the World Council of Churches. Anglican evangelicals were therefore in the ridiculous position of being in the World Council and also in a position of benevolent neutrality with respect to it.'[62]

5. The Scriptural necessity for believers and the BEC to separate from the WCC and its apostate denominations/ organisations

Dr. Lloyd-Jones thus believed that evangelical Christians should separate from apostate denominations or organisations which were members of the World Council of Churches for the sake of the defence of the Truth. This belief was based on the Scriptural commands for believers to separate and not be in fellowship with unbelievers and those who deny the Truth. We are to be in the world and to witness to unbelievers but evangelicals ought to be in visible unity with one another and not in spiritual association with those who deny the fundamentals of the Christian faith.

When can we say that a church has become apostate? Dr. Lloyd-Jones addressed this question in 1963 to members of the Westminster Fellowship:

'When do you decide that a church is apostate? Is it when the majority, and the controlling powers, in particular, are teaching error? Is it when they no longer exercise any discipline and are not even concerned about discipline and the reformation of the church?... I would suggest that the above is the very minimum, that when the main teaching, the prevailing, controlling teaching, and the power in the church has passed into the hands of those who teach error, who deny the truth, the essential truths, such a church is apostate, whatever it is, whatever it has been in the past, and whatever its own professed standards are.'[63]

Rev. Reg Burrows asked the following pertinent question about alliances with false teachers in his book *Dare to Contend!*:

'What does God say about alliances with idolaters? He made it perfectly clear to Jehoshaphat through Jehu: "Should you help the wicked and love those who hate the Lord? Because of this the wrath of the Lord is upon you" (2 Chron. 19:2). Jehoshaphat was supporting a man who worshipped Baal. He was exposing himself to heathen gods. That was what made it wicked in a spiritual sense. Such misalliances today strengthen the position of those who teach error and expose believers to compromise and heathen influence. Jehoshaphat knew the alliance was wrong, but he still went ahead.'[64]

In 1966 Rev. David P. Kingdon gave an address at the BEC conference entitled *The Biblical Attitude to Erroneous Teaching*.[65] This address examined the Biblical attitude and response to false teaching and applied Biblical principles to the current ecclesiastical situation. He examined the argument by evangelicals that '...so long as they are free to preach the gospel, they will remain in their mixed denominations. "The time to leave," they say, "is when we are cast out."' He asked whether this position could be justified by Scripture. He concluded that the answer was 'an unequivocal "No."' Rev. Kingdon explained his reasoning thus:

> 'On this view the evangelical must concede freedom to the errorist to preach his false doctrine. "So long as he lets me alone," says this type of evangelical, "I must let him alone." But...Paul would not tolerate for a moment such an idea and nor should we. Surely the Church must give a united witness to the truth. The New Testament conjoins the one body of Christ and "the unity of faith" (Eph. 4:12-13). And so must we.'

Rev. Kingdon argued that the only possible justification for evangelicals to remain in a mixed denomination was in order for them to reform the church according to the Word of God and to discipline the false teachers. However, in a mixed denomination that would inevitably lead to evangelicals being expelled from that denomination, as has indeed been the history of faithful evangelicals ejected for their Biblical stand in the past. He said:

> 'Now if it should be replied that if evangelicals attempted to exercise discipline in their mixed denominations they would be cast out, surely they have the answer: that if the situation has become so impossible that those who preach the truth are disciplined for insisting that all ministers do likewise, then evangelicals have no course open to them but to separate.'

In his 1967 BEC address entitled *Luther and His Message for Today* Dr. Lloyd-Jones argued that:

> '...not only is compromise with such people impossible for the evangelical; it is equally impossible for him to be yoked together with others in the church who deny the very elements of the Christian faith, these men who seem to deny the very being of God... who talk about the Lord Jesus Christ as a homosexual! There is no agreement— it's light and darkness! And that you should desire to hold such groups together in one territorial church, my friends, **it is a denial of the Christian faith! It is guilt by association!** If you are content to function in the same church with such people— the two groups I have mentioned— you are virtually saying that though you think you are right, that they also *may* be right- it is a possible explanation- and that, I assert, is a denial of the evangelical, the only true, faith. It is impossible.'[66]

Dr. Lloyd-Jones, commenting on this address in a sermon in 1974, said:

> 'I was criticised some eight or nine years ago for using a phrase, "guilt by association." I was told you mustn't say that. But now there is no

difficulty because the position has changed. What I saw then to be implicit has now become explicit.'[67]

Rev. David Fountain recalled that:

'Lloyd-Jones… spoke about guilt by association with regard to those who had fellowship with men in mixed denominations. He was making an important point when he said, as I clearly remember, concerning men who were in the mixed denominations: "They offer you their right hand but *to whom* are they giving their left hand?"'[68]

It is worth noting that C. H. Spurgeon made the same point regarding fellowship with error as Dr. Lloyd-Jones:

'It is our solemn conviction that where there can be no real spiritual communion there should be no pretence of fellowship. **Fellowship with known and vital error is participation in sin**.'[69]

The BEC also warned that 'for evangelical churches outwardly to remain in fellowship with the World Council of Churches or any of its associated bodies by, for instance, remaining within the doctrinally mixed denominations affiliated to it, is contrary to Scriptural principles.'[70] It pointed to the following Scriptures:

'Be ye not unequally yoked together with unbelievers: for what fellowship hath righteousness with unrighteousness? and what communion hath light with darkness? And what concord hath Christ with Belial? or what part hath he that believeth with an infidel? And what agreement hath the temple of God with idols? for ye are the temple of the living God; as God hath said, I will dwell in them, and walk in them; and I will be their God, and they shall be my people. **Wherefore come out from among them, and be ye separate**, saith the Lord, and touch not the unclean thing; and I will receive you' (2 Cor. 6:14-17).

'And I heard another voice from heaven, saying, **Come out of her, my people, that ye be not partakers of her sins, and that ye receive not of her plagues**' (Rev. 18:4).

'I marvel that ye are so soon removed from him that called you into the grace of Christ unto another gospel: Which is not another; but there be some that trouble you, and would pervert the Gospel of Christ. But though we, or an angel from heaven, preach any other gospel unto you than that which we have preached unto you, **let him be accursed**. As we said before, so say I now again. **If any man preach any other gospel unto you than that ye have received, let him be accursed**' (Gal. 1:6-9).

'Whosoever transgresseth, and abideth not in the doctrine of Christ, hath not God. He that abideth in the doctrine of Christ, he hath both the Father and the Son. If there come any unto you, and bring not this doctrine, **receive him not into your house, neither bid him God speed: For he that biddeth him God speed is partaker of his evil deeds**' (2 John 9-11).

'Now I beseech you, brethren, **mark them which cause divisions and offences contrary to the doctrine which ye have learned; and avoid them**' (Rom. 16:17).

'If any man teach otherwise, and consent not to wholesome words, even the words of our Lord Jesus Christ, and to the doctrine which is according to godliness; he is proud, knowing nothing but doting about questions and strifes of words, whereof cometh envy, strife, railings, evil surmisings, Perverse disputings of men of corrupt minds, and destitute of the truth, supposing that gain is godliness: **from such withdraw thyself**' (1 Tim. 6:3-5).

The BEC saw that if believers fail to follow these Scriptural commands there are two grievous results. Firstly that 'the Gospel is compromised, if not denied, since such is an attempt to achieve organisational union at the expense of vital Christian truths,'[71] and secondly that 'the expression of a true evangelical unity in a fellowship at church level is grievously hindered.'[72] The BEC was thus 'fundamentally different from the modern ecumenical movement [in which] the unique Gospel of Scripture is not seen as essential for church unity.'[73]

It was therefore BEC policy that evangelical churches which were allied with those who deny the Truth were unable to become members, since the Council believed that 'by identifying with a church body which grants equal status to false gospels their own testimony is distorted.'[74] Furthermore, the BEC said that this was such an important principle for the sake of the Gospel that it was a matter of conscience that they could not allow churches with alliances to the WCC to join them:

'The EA [Evangelical Alliance]... does accept Gospel churches irrespective of the ecumenical involvement of their church group. By contrast, **the BEC comprises only churches which cannot, on grounds of conscience, identify with any such ecumenical involvement**.'[75]

To sum up, the British Evangelical Council was 'a Council of evangelical churches within the British Isles which **actively dissociate[d] themselves from the World Council of Churches and its member-bodies** so that in fellowship together they [made] an **uncompromised witness to Biblical truths** and safeguard[ed] their freedom to worship and witness,'[76] according to primary Biblical truth. As the BEC stressed, 'the need for this will become the more obvious and urgent as contrary ecumenical pressures build up.'[77]

6. *Affinity's departure from Scriptural and key BEC principles of separation from the WCC and its apostate denominations/organisations*

In 1984 the then General Secretary of the BEC, Alan Gibson, re-published the *Official Statement: Attitude to Ecumenicity* in the BEC newsletter, declaring that 'The present Executive Council wishes to indicate their unchanged convictions about these vital issues by re-publishing exactly the same statement.'[78]

However, following the Doctor's death in 1981 men who held to the same Biblical principles as Dr. Lloyd-Jones and the BEC were witnessing a drift amongst evangelicals away from the principles of separation from the Ecumenical Movement.

In 1984 Rev. T. Omri Jenkins[79] wrote an article entitled *Drifting,*[80] in order to warn evangelicals about the 'woolly thinking about Rome and its liberal and modernistic counterparts [and the] disturbing... drift which seems to be developing within circles once fully committed to a firm stance against them.'[81] He warned that:

> 'It is common experience that every institution worth having, or position worth holding, has to be actively and constantly maintained against attack in one form or another. Oftentimes the attack is overt and furious, and for those reasons can be easily recognised and resisted. A far greater danger lies in the more subtle drifting which occurs, sometimes within, when developments and their trends are not discerned or, for one reason or another, are disregarded...
>
> Nearly a century ago Mr. Spurgeon had to stand all but alone in the 'down-grade controversy!' This was not because there were no other good evangelicals in the Baptist churches of his day; there were very many, but for one reason or another they allowed the situation to drift, which is what it did until it hit the rocks!'[82]

History has shown that Rev. T. O. Jenkins' warning went unheeded. The drift continued and in 2004 the BEC was re-named as *Affinity* under a new 'Director,'[83] with an agenda to 'develop the Anglican dimension.'[84] Rev. Roger Fay,[85] editor of the *Evangelical Times,* reporting on the launch warned that:

> 'No reference was made during the hour-long press conference to former leaders of the BEC movement, such as E. J. Poole-Connor and D. M. Lloyd-Jones. Minimal definition was given to Affinity's doctrinal stance...'[86]

Rev. John Thackway,[87] editor of the *Bible League Quarterly*, warned that:

> 'For many people, Affinity's criteria for fellowship and co-operation will
> be wider than is Biblical and more inclusive than is acceptable.'[88]

This prediction was fulfilled in 2006 when the Director of Affinity announced in the Affinity newsletter that the organisation was welcoming two churches as members from denominations belonging to the WCC: one from the United Reformed Church and the other belonging to the Baptist Union.[89] Neither of these churches were intending to leave their doctrinally mixed denominations. As demonstrated above, this was a complete departure from the fundamental principles of the BEC as set out in their *Official Statement: Attitude to Ecumenicity*. As the Rev. Michael Buss, a former editor of the *BEC Newsletter* said in 1970:

> '...it would be utterly anomalous if evangelical churches involved locally
> in the ecumenical movement and/or committed denominationally to it
> were to join a Council committed to unity in the Gospel alone.'[90]

The Affinity website reveals that the organisation has now embraced Anglicans. Oak Hill Theological College, which trains men and women for ministry in the Church of England, has been made an Affinity Corporate Partner. The Yorkshire Gospel Partnership and the Midlands Gospel Partnership[91] are also Corporate Partners, the former including an Anglican congregation, and the latter including a significant number of Anglican churches.

As previously discussed (p.16), Dr. Lloyd-Jones had allied himself with the BEC rather than the Evangelical Alliance, specifically to make a clear stand apart from the WCC and its mixed denominations. His comments regarding the BEC's separated stand are very helpful when considering the changes in Affinity regarding the introduction of member churches belonging to the WCC through their denominations. In his address entitled *True and False Religion* Dr. Lloyd-Jones explained why it was important to take the BEC's stand against the WCC:

> 'Why this BEC? Why not join the other evangelicals? Because they are
> mixed up with infidels and sceptics and denials of the truth. They are!
> Every other evangelical organisation that I am aware of consists of those
> who are mixed up in their denominations with people who deny the truth
> as much as the prophets of Baal did. They deny the deity of Christ!...
> Now this is the tragedy. But, you see, if you protest, if you stand out and
> say, "I cannot belong to this," you are regarded as a troubler in Israel,
> someone who is causing disagreement amongst friends. If you today
> make a plea for evangelical unity you will be charged with dividing
> evangelicals. The man who stands for the truth is the troubler of Israel.'[92]

In his address *The Sword and the Song* Dr. Lloyd-Jones stated:

> 'We, who belong to the BEC... are not content to be an evangelical wing in a mixed community... Furthermore, we are quite clear about the importance of the purity of the church. We are separatists. We are nonconformists. We are dissenters. We do not believe that the institution comes first and that it must be preserved, even at the expense of tolerating denials of essential truth. We believe in the purity of the Word preached and in the regular administration of the sacraments. And we believe in discipline in those respects at the same time.'[93]

Although the BEC had welcomed an Anglican church[94] into membership in 1987, the minister of this church, Rev. Reg Burrows, had made it plain that he could not remain indefinitely within the denomination due to its apostasy. The BEC newsletter stated that:

> 'They have made it clear that they are not willing to remain indefinitely in a church which tolerates heresy. We would be unable to receive a church which sees the only saving Gospel merely as one of several equally valid options in the body where they are content to remain at all costs...'[95]

Indeed, in 1994, after faithfully and earnestly contending for the Faith and pleading with other Anglican evangelicals to do the same,[96] the Rev. Reg Burrows seceded from the Anglican Church.

Rev. Vernon Higham,[97] Dr. Lloyd-Jones' close friend in the ministry, has warned:

> 'Unity with Anglicans is in the end unity with Rome. They are avowedly heading that way.'[98]

C. H. Spurgeon had resigned from the Baptist Union in 1887 stating the following principles which were in keeping with those of Dr. Lloyd-Jones and the BEC principles as stated above:

> 'Complicity with error will take from the best of men the power to enter any successful protest against it.'[99] 'As soon as I saw, or thought I saw, that error had become firmly established, I did not deliberate, but quitted the body at once. Since then my counsel has been "Come out from among them" (2 Cor. 6:17)... I have felt that no protest could be equal to that of distinct separation from known evil.'[100]

The BEC's *Official Statement* is not published on the Affinity website.[101] Furthermore, the Affinity *Mission Statement* and the information entitled

Why does Affinity exist? have no mention of any stand whatsoever against the Ecumenical Movement; they simply focus on 'the unity of Christ's Church' in partnerships with evangelicals and, as we have seen, this is apparently regardless of their links with the WCC.

Indeed, in his article *Latest Moves in Evangelical Unity* in 2006, Rev. Nigel Lacey[102] pointed out that 'the Affinity literature is unambiguous in declaring that Affinity is not the BEC but something new.'[103] What then is the purpose of this new organisation? Rev. Nigel Lacey concluded:

> 'We must accept that it is wrong to hold hands with those who are already in league with reprobates and rejecters of the Truth. It would appear that Affinity takes a different view and that the reason for dissolving the BEC and launching Affinity is to avoid limitations and restrictions upon this kind of fellowship.'[104]

Affinity's fundamental departure from BEC key principles has been the cause of immense sadness to those men who stood with Dr. Lloyd-Jones and the BEC in its early days. They have seen the very principles they stood for in order to make a clear and strong stand against the Ecumenical Movement overturned and indeed 'forgotten.'

The late J. Elwyn Davies,[105] Chairman of the BEC from 1969-72 and one of the chief founders of the Evangelical Movement of Wales (EMW), stated that:

> '... in that [the EMW] was already pursuing a similar objective within Wales, the Movement in 1967 sought affiliation as a constituent member of the British Evangelical Council.'[106]

J. Elwyn Davies stated the following regarding the 'conditions of affiliation' of churches to the EMW:

> 'The only conditions of affiliation are that they seek to confine membership to true believers, that their doctrinal standards coincide with the Doctrinal Belief of the Movement, **and that they are not compromised by association with a doctrinally mixed Council of Churches.**'[107]

Indeed in 1983 J. Elwyn Davies said that he trusted and prayed that there would never come a time when the questions and visions of the BEC in its early days would be laid aside by evangelicals.[108]

May the principles of these faithful men be resurrected in a bold stand against the Ecumenical Movement in our day.

7. Dr. Lloyd-Jones' and the BEC's plea for evangelicals to separate from doctrinally mixed denominations

'God's people have no right to remain in any Babylon'

Like John Calvin, both the BEC and Dr. Lloyd-Jones made the distinction between primary and secondary truths. The fundamentals of the Faith are those truths which *all* true believers do believe, such as the inerrancy of Scripture, man's utter ruin through the Fall, God's plan of redemption and the Person and work of the Lord Jesus Christ. 'Secondary truths' were those important truths which, nevertheless, true believers sometimes disagree upon.

It should be noted that Dr. Lloyd-Jones did not teach that secondary truths were unimportant. The New Evangelical views secondary truths as 'not important,'[109] perhaps even believing that it is divisive to teach, discuss or defend such Biblical teaching. However, the Apostle Paul stated that he had 'not shunned to declare... *all* the counsel of God' (Acts 20:27), and Dr. Lloyd-Jones and other Biblically-based evangelicals have likewise preached on secondary issues such as baptism and the second coming of the Lord Jesus Christ.

Both the BEC and Dr. Lloyd-Jones believed that evangelicals ought to have fellowship at church level with other true believers who were united in their Gospel beliefs but who nevertheless disagreed where secondary matters were concerned. They were not isolationist in principle but as demonstrated above, where the true Gospel was being denied, they believed that evangelicals ought not to be seen to be in fellowship with error and compromise. Therefore Anglican, Methodist, United Reformed and Baptist Union churches were not permitted to join because of their membership of the WCC. It was hoped that evangelicals who belonged to the WCC would free themselves of their denominational association with it.

Dr. Lloyd-Jones and the BEC pleaded with evangelicals to separate from doctrinally mixed denominations and instead come into fellowship with true believers for the sake of the Gospel and Christian witness to the Truth to those outside of Christ. In 1972, at the Fellowship of Independent Evangelical Churches (FIEC)[110] Annual Assembly, Dr. Lloyd-Jones gave an address entitled *The Call to Liberty*[111] (on Deut. 6:23) in which he argued that believers have no spiritual freedom in a mixed denomination with false teachers:

> '...with a mixed multitude you have no freedom. If you're involved with people who deny essential aspects of the Truth— if you're in a mixed denomination where some deny the very Being of God and others the deity of Christ and most of the cardinal articles of the Christian faith —

how can you enjoy freedom in worship? How can you pray with a man who denies the deity of the Lord? I say it's impossible! It just cannot be done. Or how can you be free in your worship and in your conduct of your Christian life if you're always having to consider that if you say something you may be offending a brother minister in the same denomination or something of that kind? How can you be free when you're always having to accommodate and always having to be wary lest you cause some offence? My dear friends, these things are impossible! There is the conflict between the institution and the Spirit— between the letter and the Spirit, and it is because God wants His people to be free, as the Apostle Paul puts it in that ringing phrase... [in] the Epistle to the Galatians: "Brethren, ye have been called unto liberty" (Gal 5:13), and the call of the Gospel is always a great call to liberty...'

What was Dr. Lloyd-Jones' view on such a situation?

> 'God's people have no right to remain in any Babylon. They may have comfort, but their business, I say, is not to belong there but to *come out* and to enjoy the liberty wherewith Christ has set them free! So that the first thing that has to happen to people in this condition is that they have to come forth...'[112]

Evangelicals determined to remain in the mixed denominations often refer to the original paper constitution of their Church and use the 'in-it-to-win-it' argument. For example, evangelicals in the Church of England point to the *Thirty-Nine Articles* as justification for their remaining in a mixed denomination.

However, in his 1966 address *Evangelical Unity: An Appeal,* Dr. Lloyd-Jones reminded evangelicals that the Church is not a 'paper church' but consists of living people:

> 'The church, surely, is not a paper definition. I am sorry, I cannot accept the view that a church consists of articles or of a confession of faith. A church does not consist of the Thirty-Nine Articles. A church does not consist of the Westminster Confession of Faith. A church does not consist of the Savoy Declaration. A church consists of *living people.* You cannot have a church without *living people.* You can have a paper constitution with a majority in that church denying that very constitution. That is no longer a church as I see it.'[113]

Dr. Lloyd-Jones described the idea of infiltrating and reforming apostate churches as 'midsummer madness'[114] and pointed to the evidence of history and to the necessity of obeying Biblical principles:

'When a church is apostate or refuses repeated attempts to discipline those in error on these matters, you cannot reform her. This is the testimony of history. You must try to do so; you must try to get discipline to be exercised. If they will not do so... separate yourself from them and "be not partaker of their evil deeds."'[115]

In 1963 the BEC published a booklet written by T. H. Bendor-Samuel, one of the early leaders of the FIEC, in which the involvement of evangelicals in the mixed denominations and hence in the Ecumenical Movement was examined. In this booklet T. H. Bendor-Samuel said:

'Within the ranks of evangelicals are those who advocate participation in the ecumenical movement in order to seek to influence it from within. "If we are uneasy about things in the movement we should show it a better way, and we can only do so from within." Such is the argument... The mixed character of the World Council is only a reflection of the mixed nature of many of our churches. There are evangelicals in them; have they prevented the drift towards liberalism or ritualism? But the issue must be settled from Scripture, not from mere policy. Such passages as Galatians 1:9, already quoted, teach separation, not involvement. Paul did not "seek to share the insights" of the Judaisers. He denounced their teaching as being destructive of the Gospel, and he did so in the strongest possible terms. Here are the Scriptures: "What fellowship hath righteousness with unrighteousness, and what concord hath light with darkness? ...Be ye separate, saith the Lord" (2 Cor. 6: 14-18). "Withdraw from every brother that walketh disorderly and not after the tradition which he received from us" (2 Thess. 3:6). "Receive him not into your house" (2 John 10). This is not participation with those who teach false doctrine, but separation from them.
...It is sin to separate ourselves from our fellow believers without proper reason, but it is also sin to be unfaithful to the Gospel that has been committed to our trust, and to connive in teaching and movements that are destructive of the faith, and so of the souls of men. There are times when every loyal Christian has to say, "Stand thou on that side, for on this stand I."'[116]

Dr. Lloyd-Jones was aware of the financial or family difficulties that men could have in leaving their denominations but he stressed that the true Christian has always had problems, sometimes grievous ones, and yet 'they were not daunted; they went on; they believed, they knew; they would rather die than not stand for the Truth.'[117] The BEC also recognised these problems and was 'concerned to offer practical help' so it set up a fund in order to help individuals and churches who were seceding for the sake of the Gospel.

8. The necessary division at church level between evangelicals, inside and outside of the Ecumenical Movement, for the sake of the Gospel

As we have seen, both Dr. Lloyd-Jones and the BEC saw that the Scriptures command true believers not to have fellowship with unbelievers, and hence believers ought not to belong to denominations propagating false gospels. As some true evangelicals remain in their mixed denominations, how then ought evangelicals to relate to other evangelical individuals and churches which remain in the doctrinally mixed denominations?

Both the Doctor and the BEC believed that evangelicals should continue in private fellowship with believers in mixed denominations, but not have fellowship with them on the church level. They believed that evangelical churches ought not to have fellowship or association with other evangelical churches belonging to the mixed denominations. This was in order to make a clear stand for the Truth and so that believers and unbelievers would be clear as to the true Gospel.

The BEC statement said the following:

> 'It is, of course, an unhappy thing that brethren who are truly one in Christ should yet be divided at church level from each other on account of differing attitudes to the Ecumenical Movement. For that very reason it is necessary for us to state our deep conviction that what is at stake is no mere interpretation of Scripture but the Gospel itself. We totally reject the plea that the issues raised are secondary matters. They concern the very nature, purity and defence of the Gospel itself, and in the foreseeable future, according to present indications, even the freedom to preach that Gospel without compromise. The gathering momentum and increasingly obvious direction of the present Ecumenical Movement already clearly demonstrates that Scriptural justification can no longer be found even for neutrality toward it, let alone active participation in it.'[118]

Rev. Paul Bassett, a member of the Westminster Fellowship for many years in the time of Dr. Lloyd-Jones, confirmed that Dr. Lloyd-Jones was of the same mind as the BEC on this matter. He stated that:

> 'The Doctor taught that we should have fellowship at a private level with evangelicals in mixed denominations but *not* at church level.'[119]

Dr. Christopher Catherwood, Dr. Lloyd-Jones' grandson, agreed that Dr. Lloyd-Jones had no church level fellowship with men in the mixed denominations and added that Lloyd-Jones:

'continued to have private fellowship with his Anglican friends such as John Gwyn-Thomas[120] and Philip Edgcumbe Hughes,[121] but on the church level *absolutely nothing.*'[122]

Rev. Harry Waite,[123] a member of the Westminster Fellowship[124] in the time of Dr. Lloyd-Jones, has said:

'Dr. Lloyd-Jones remained in private fellowship with his friends in the doctrinally mixed denominations but his policy was no church level fellowship. Whilst the Doctor would preach for sinners anywhere,[125] he would never invite men from the mixed denominations into *his* pulpit. He wanted to make his position and the message of the Gospel very clear.'[126]

Indeed, in an address to ministers in the Westminster Fellowship, Dr. Lloyd-Jones said this:

'We are to have private fellowship with those who associate with the Ecumenical Movement but not fellowship on a church level; these have left *us* and this perpetuates the confusion. So how do you influence compromised evangelicals if you leave them? By *clarifying our own position* we help them most.'[127]

This position of no church level fellowship with evangelicals belonging to doctrinally mixed denominations was also adopted by C. H. Spurgeon in order to make a clear stand for the Truth:

'That I might not stultify my testimony I have cut myself clear of those who err from the Faith, **and even from those who associate with them.**'[128]

Rev. T. Omri Jenkins, who was a member of the Westminster Fellowship with Dr. Lloyd-Jones, was known to be of the same opinion as the Doctor[129] regarding secondary separation[130] for the sake of the Gospel. In his article *Drifting*[131] he stated the following:

'The main attack on Bible Christianity in the second half of the twentieth century has come from Ecumenism, and while many evangelicals have taken a clear stand against it, others have felt they can live with it and still retain their own evangelical convictions...'[132]

Regarding division between evangelicals inside and outside of the Ecumenical Movement he concludes:

'That these two positions should result in divisions among evangelicals is *regrettable* but *surely unavoidable*.'[133]

Rev. T. Omri Jenkins argued, as the BEC and Dr. Lloyd-Jones had done, that this necessary separation between evangelicals was 'over principles, not personalities' and for the sake of the Gospel:

'...let it at least be recognised that those of us who will stand and will not keep quiet about it do so out of heart concern, without rancour or animus... Our considered purpose is to contend for principles which for us are ultimately of the essence of the Faith and in this we will persist with the hope and prayer that the drift we see may be arrested.'[134]

Rev. T. Omri Jenkins' principles of secondary separation were illustrated when he was compelled to write to the FIEC Assembly in 1984 in order to 'express [his] grave disquiet' that they had invited an Anglican to speak at the Assembly. Rev. Jenkins acknowledged Dick Lucas' reputation of 'thorough evangelical faith' but warned that:

'He is a continuing member of an organised religion which is compromised to the utmost and is avowedly heading for unity with Rome.'[135]

Rev. Robert Sheehan, who was a member of the Westminster Fellowship with Dr. Lloyd-Jones, commented that the stand regarding the compromised evangelicals in mixed denominations had been 'no separation' in the late 1950s and 'public but not private separation' in the late 1960s.'[136] Commenting on the invitation issued by the FIEC to an Anglican remaining in a mixed denomination to speak at their Assembly, he states that this was 'an essential rejection of the position advocated by E. J. Poole-Connor, Dr. Lloyd-Jones and the British Evangelical Council in the late 1960s.'[137]

It should be noted that some evangelicals, including Dr. Peter Masters, go a little further than Dr. Lloyd-Jones by arguing that evangelicals should practise church level *and* private level separation from compromised evangelicals. Dr. Peter Masters expounds his arguments in the booklet entitled *Stand for the Truth;*[138] these are based on 2 Thessalonians 3:6:

'Now we command you, brethren, in the name of our Lord Jesus Christ, that ye withdraw yourselves from every brother that walketh disorderly, and not after the tradition which he received of us.'

Dr. Lloyd Jones' position towards evangelicals in doctrinally mixed denominations was also apparent in the Westminster Fellowship's conditions for membership[139] which were reconstituted in response to the threat of Ecumenism in 1967. The new principles of membership were aimed at recognising 'the need for true evangelical unity at church level.' Anglican men who would not commit themselves to secession were then excluded from the reconstituted Fellowship as the principles stated that separation from denominations linked to the World Council of Churches was 'inevitable.' The principles were the following:

1. We are all conservative evangelicals whose first loyalty is to the conservative evangelical faith, rather than to any inherited traditional position.
2. We are all already dissatisfied with the denominational position, and are grieved with what appears to us to be compromise on the part of many evangelicals in the doctrinally mixed denominations.
3. We see no hope whatsoever of winning such doctrinally mixed denominations to an evangelical position.
4. We are calling on all evangelicals to come together on an uncompromising Gospel basis, which involves us in opposition to the Ecumenical Movement because of its obvious overall trends.
5. Those who are at present in denominations linked with the World Council of Churches are agreed that separation from such denominations is inevitable, and seek to know the mind of God concerning the steps which they should take.
6. Recognising the urgency of the times, we desire to express our evangelical unity by meeting in this fellowship, and to discuss prayerfully together the principles upon which our unity may be expressed at church level, moving in the direction of a fellowship of evangelical churches.

Dr. Lloyd-Jones and the BEC understood and believed that it was right for men leaving mixed denominations to have time to first counsel their congregations as to the Scriptural principles of separation from error. Rev. Graham Harrison, for example, left the Baptist Union when it became apparent that one of its leaders was not going to be disciplined for his blasphemy. Before leaving the Baptist Union, he first contended for the Truth and explained to others why it was necessary that he should come out. In a conversation with the author in 2007 Rev. Graham Harrison explained the Doctor's position on both secondary separation and seceding from mixed denominations:

'The Doctor continued in fellowship with men in situations like myself who, though we remained in the Baptist Union or mixed denominations, were doing so for a time in order to contend for the Truth before leaving.

The Doctor did not remain in church level fellowship with those men who were determined never to leave their denominations. With such men he continued in private fellowship but had no fellowship with them on a church level. He did not believe in evangelicals being seen to be in fellowship with apostate denominations and it was his heartfelt desire that good evangelical men would leave such associations for the sake of the Gospel and true evangelical unity.'[140]

Rev. Robert Sheehan said this regarding Dr. Lloyd-Jones:

'He respected the problems of those who took time over their secession, as he wanted them to bring their churches with them. He even encouraged some men to go into churches in mixed denominations if those churches were looking for leadership and were able to be taught the principles of secession.'[141]

The BEC shared the Doctor's beliefs and sympathy with men intending to secede from compromised denominations:

'…we would be most anxious to declare our full sympathy with those who share these convictions but who have yet to take active steps in this matter though waiting upon the Lord for His clear leading as to exactly how and when they are to dissociate themselves from the denominations that are actively involved in the Ecumenical Movement. What we deeply regret is that so many of our evangelical brethren now seem to be committed to such definite involvement. For ourselves, for the reasons stated above, we have felt compelled to withdraw, or stay apart, from the World Council of Churches, and to seek active fellowship with each other at church level.'[142]

Like Dr. Lloyd-Jones, the BEC did not advocate withdrawal from private fellowship with evangelicals who remained in their apostate denominations:

'We wish to affirm, however, our sincere desire to remain in personal fellowship with all who are truly Christ's. Though we feel compelled to let our fellow-evangelicals who do not at present agree with us know our convictions in these matters, we desire to do so in Christian love. This is not least because we know from personal experience the cost and heart-searching of applying Scriptural principles to ecumenical issues and because of our deep conviction that reformation according to God's Word seems so often to be a Biblical prerequisite for a visitation of the Holy Spirit in revival, which is our greatest need today.'[143]

The *Official Statement: Attitude to Ecumenicity* therefore ended with a call for evangelicals to apply Scriptural principles to ecumenical issues and with the hope that the Lord would once again revive His people.

In the light of the situation that pertains today in Evangelicalism and of the possible impending emergence of the Ecumenical World Church, there is therefore an urgent need for the words of Dr. Lloyd-Jones which condemn the non-separating, non-contending ethos of New Evangelicalism to be heeded:

> '"Beloved, when I gave all diligence to write unto you of the common salvation, it was needful for me to write unto you, and exhort you that ye should earnestly contend for the faith which was once delivered unto the saints" (Jude 3). Here we are given a stirring call to the defence of the faith. Such a call is not popular today. It is not popular today even in some evangelical circles. People will tell you that it is all "too negative." They continually urge that we must keep on giving positive truth. They will tell us that we must not argue and we must never condemn. But we must ask, How can you fight if you are ever afraid of wounding an enemy? How can you rouse sleeping fellow-warriors with smooth words? God forbid that we find ourselves at the bar of judgment and face the charge that we contracted out from love of ease or for fear of man, or that we failed to do our duty in the great fight of the faith. We *must* – we *must* fight for the faith in these momentous times.'[144]

9. *Conclusion*

We thank God for the love, unity and fellowship that *does* exist between churches throughout the UK who love the Truth and are not ecumenically compromised. It is clear, however, that being part of Affinity will now bring churches into association with churches belonging to the WCC and the Ecumenical Movement. Hence the clear, separated and uncompromised stand of the BEC in its early days, both *against* the Ecumenical Movement and *for* true Biblical unity, has sadly been lost. As T. H. Bendor-Samuel once said:

> '... the weakness of the church today is no mere matter of relationship between believers, nor is it only a question of disunity. It springs from a spiritual state, not just an organizational one. The sin of departing from the truth as it is in Christ, of infidelity and apostasy, this is what has robbed us of our strength. Church unity that ignores this, and even hastens it, can bring us no cure. To attribute the church's present malady to her disunion is a palpably false diagnosis, for it ignores the deeper and graver disease, the unbelief of professing Christians.'[145]

It is our hope and prayer that the spirit of men like the Apostle Paul, Martin Luther, John Knox, Hugh Latimer, Charles H. Spurgeon and Dr. Martyn Lloyd-Jones, men who were prepared to earnestly contend for the Faith and even die for it if necessary, would be restored to evangelicals today.

It is vital that the principles outlined in the BEC's *Official Statement: Attitude to Ecumenicity,* which were formed on Biblical principles, should once again be remembered and upheld, as they are the only means of a faithful and strong stance against Ecumenism and Rome.

Endnotes

[1] E. J. Poole-Connor (1872-1962) was a founder and leader of both the British Evangelical Council and the Fellowship of Independent Evangelical Churches.

[2] Dr. Martyn Lloyd-Jones (1899-1981) was a Welshman and one of the greatest preachers of the 20th Century. He was the minister of Westminster Chapel in London from 1939 to 1968, working alongside Rev. G. Campbell Morgan (1863-1945). For further information on the life of Dr. Lloyd-Jones please refer to Iain H. Murray's biography (in two volumes) published by the Banner of Truth Trust.

[3] D. Martyn Lloyd-Jones *How to Safeguard the Future* (1969). Printed in *Knowing the Times: Addresses Delivered on Various Occasions 1942-1977* (The Banner of Truth Trust, 1989, pp.280-281). This address was given at a thanksgiving service during the fiftieth Annual Conference of the Inter-Varsity Fellowship, and Dr. Lloyd-Jones is quoting from the second paragraph of W. R. Inge's *The Victorian Age* (Cambridge University Press, 1922).

[4] D. Martyn Lloyd-Jones *Sound an Alarm* (Oct 29, 1969). This address was delivered at the BEC conference at Westminster Chapel. Printed in *Unity in Truth* (Evangelical Press, 1991, edited by Hywel Rees Jones, p.67).

[5] Ibid, p.66-67.

[6] Ibid, p.67.

[7] 'Contemporary Christian Music' (CCM) is a genre of modern pop music which is lyrically concerned with the Christian faith. The lyrics are often heavily ecumenical. It originated from the 'Jesus Movement' of the late 1960s and early 1970s. See Wikipedia.

[8] See David Cloud's *Contemporary Christian Music: Some questions answered and some warnings given* (Way of Life Literature, 2006) for evidence that CCM is the music used at ecumenical conferences. For example, p.31 states:
'CCM was the music of the largest ecumenical Charismatic conference New Orleans '87... [and] the preferred music of the 40,000 ecumenical-Charismatics in attendance. Approximately 40 different denominations and groups came together under one roof... including roughly 20,000 Roman Catholics. Roman Catholic priest Tom Forrest delivered the closing message and brought the mixed multitude to their feet when he called for unity. "We must reach the world," he cried, "and we must reach it the only way we can reach it; we must reach it TOGETHER!" At those words the crowd became ecstatic, leaping to their feet, shouting, stomping, speaking in tongues, dancing... At the book sales area in New Orleans one could purchase Rosary beads and a Madonna to assist in one's prayers to Mary. A Catholic Mass was held every morning during the conference. The music that held all of this confusion together was CCM. Youth Explosion '87 was held at the same time, and 5,000 young people were bombarded with a steady diet of unscriptural teaching, ecumenism, testimonies by sports stars and entertainment figures, and "Christian" rock music.'

[9] Comment by Dr. Peter Masters in the postscript to the revised version of Rev. David Fountain's book *Contending for the Faith: E. J. Poole-Connor - A prophet amidst the sweeping changes in English evangelicalism* (The Wakeman Trust, 2005, p.173).

[10] 'The Emerging Church... is a [new] Christian movement that crosses a number of theological boundaries: participants can be described as Protestant, post-Protestant, Catholic, evangelical, post-evangelical, liberal, post liberal, conservative, post-conservative, Anabaptist, Adventist, Reformed, Charismatic, neo-Charismatic, and post Charismatic'(Wikipedia).

[11] See Iain H. Murray's *Evangelicalism Divided* (Banner of Truth Trust, 2000) for further information on 'New Evangelicalism.'

[12] John Monroe "Monk" Parker (1909-1994) was a Baptist evangelist and teacher at Bob Jones University and General Director of Baptist World Mission.

[13] Harold John Ockenga (1905-1985) was a Congregational minister who served for many years as pastor of Park Street Church in Boston, Massachusetts, and one of the leaders of the 'Neo-Evangelicalism.'

[14] Monroe Parker, *Frontline* (Jul-Aug, 1991, p. 25). Quoted in David Cloud's *Evangelicals and Rome: The Ecumenical One World Church* (Way of Life Literature, 2006, pp.10-11).

[15] H. J. Ockenga's foreword to *The Battle for the Bible* by Harold Lindsell (Calvary Chapel Publishing, 2008).

[16] H. J. Ockenga's Press release (December 8th, 1957). Quoted in David Cloud's *New Evangelicalism* (Way of Life Literature, 2006, p.56).

[17] 'The New Age movement is a Western spiritual movement that developed in the second half of the 20th century. Its central precepts have been described as "drawing on both Eastern and Western spiritual and metaphysical traditions and infusing them with influences from self-help and motivational psychology, holistic health, parapsychology, consciousness research and quantum physics"'(Wikipedia). 'Positive thinking' and 'positive confession' are key New Age doctrines which have gained a stronghold in churches. See David Cloud's *The New Age Tower of Babel* (Way of Life Literature, 2008, pp.42-43).

[18] D. Martyn Lloyd-Jones *Sound an Alarm* (Oct 29, 1969). This address was delivered at the BEC conference at Westminster Chapel. Printed in *Unity in Truth* (Evangelical Press, 1991, edited by Hywel Rees Jones, pp.74-75).

[19] D. Martyn Lloyd-Jones *The Basis of Christian Unity*. This was the substance of two addresses given to the Westminster Ministers' Fellowship in June, 1962. Printed in *Knowing the Times* (The Banner of Truth Trust, 1989, p.157).

[20] John Murray (1898-1975) was a Christian minister and theologian of the Reformed faith. He was Professor of Systematic Theology at Westminster Theological Seminary (USA) from 1930-1967 and minister in the Orthodox Presbyterian Church from 1937 until his death.

[21] Prof. John Murray *Co-operation in Evangelism: Can we co-operate without compromise?* (British Evangelical Council, 1965, p.11).

[22] J. Sidlow Baxter (1903-1999) was born in Australia and raised in Lancashire. He was a pastor in England and Scotland.

[23] J. Sidlow Baxter *Mark These Men* (Kregel Publications, 1992, p.17).

[24] Robert Haldane (1764-1842) was a Scottish preacher.

[25] Robert Haldane's *Fear of Controversy*, written in 1874, can be found at: http://www.pbministries.org/Theology/Haldane/Robert/fear_of_controversy.htm

[26] Rev. Geoff Thomas has been the minister of Alfred Place Baptist Church in Aberystwyth, Wales, since 1965, and he presently serves as an Associate Editor of the Banner of Truth magazine.

[27] On February 24th 2012, Rev. Geoff Thomas kindly agreed that this statement (which originated in an e-mail to the author on January 21st 2012) could be printed.

[28] C. H. Spurgeon's sermon on Matthew 26:10 entitled *Something Done for Jesus* (Metropolitan Tabernacle Pulpit, Volume 36, No. 2126).

[29] D. Martyn Lloyd-Jones *The Christian and Persecution* in Vol. 1 of *Studies in the Sermon on the Mount* (IVP, 1959, pp.136).

[30] C. H. Spurgeon's sermon on Romans 8:14 entitled *The Leading Of The Spirit, The Secret Token of the Sons of God* (Metropolitan Tabernacle Pulpit, Volume 21, No. 1220).

[31] Ernest D. Pickering (1928-2000) was the pastor of several churches in the USA, served at the Baptist Bible College in Pennsylvania, the Central Baptist Theological Seminary in Minneapolis and the Baptist World Mission.

[32] Ernest Pickering has described 'young evangelicals' as: '... younger persons who have imbibed the general philosophy of the older "new evangelicals," but are more radical' (*Biblical Separation: The Struggle for a Pure Church*, Regular Baptist Press, 1979, p.131).

[33] Ernest Pickering *Biblical Separation: The Struggle for a Pure Church* (Regular Baptist Press, 1979, p.136).

[34] David Fountain *E. J. Poole-Connor: Contender for the Faith* (H. E. Walter, 1966). This edition has been revised and renamed: *Contending for the Faith: E. J. Poole-Connor - A prophet amidst the sweeping changes in English evangelicalism* (The Wakeman Trust, 2005, p.159).

[35] *BEC Newsletter*, No. 6, February 1971.

[36] Iain H. Murray *D. Martyn Lloyd-Jones: The Fight of Faith: 1939-1981* (The Banner of Truth Trust, 1990, p.504).

[37] C. H. Spurgeon *Sermons* (Vol. 10, pp. 322-3). Quoted in David Cloud's *Evangelicals and Rome: The Ecumenical One World Church* (Way of Life Literature, 2006, p.9).

[38] Martin Luther *Luther's Works* (Weimar Edition. Briefwechsel [Correspondence], vol. 3, pp.81f).

[39] D. Martyn Lloyd-Jones *Evangelical Unity: An Appeal* (18-19 Oct, 1966). Address given at the Second National Assembly of Evangelicals. Published in *Knowing the Times* (The Banner of Truth Trust, 1989, p.248).

[40] E. J. Poole-Connor *The World Council of Churches: Whence... and Whither?* (The British Evangelical Council, 1967, p.10).

[41] Hugh Latimer *Hugh Latimer Works* (vol. 1, p.487). Quoted in J.C. Ryle's *Five English Reformers* (The Banner of Truth Trust, 1960, p.118).

[42] British Evangelical Council *Official Statement: Attitude to Ecumenicity* (BEC Newsletter, June, 1968).

[43] Ibid.

[44] Gjerding and Kinnamon *No longer strangers: A resource for women and worship* (Geneva: WCC Publications, 1983).

[45] David Cloud *The World Council of Churches* (Way of Life Literature, 2001, p.12).

[46] The World Council of Churches, 9th Assembly (Porto Alegre, Brazil, February 14th-23rd, 2006).

[47] Parker T. Williamson *Peace rally prays to no one in particular* (The Presbyterian Layman, Feb. 22nd, 2006).

[48] *The Mystery of Salvation* (Doctrine Commission of the Church of England, 1995, p.122).

[49] Kevin Ranaghan (1940-) is a Catholic Charismatic who has aided communication between Catholics and Protestants from Pentecostal, mainline, and evangelical streams of Christianity, who were experiencing the Charismatic phenomena (Wikipedia).

[50] Jamie Buckingham (1933-1992) was a popular Charismatic speaker and writer. He pastored the Tabernacle Church in Florida, was a consultant for Wycliffe Bible Translators and was the president of the National Leadership Conference. He began his ministry as a Southern Baptist pastor but later became a Pentecostal.

[51] Jamie Buckingham's statement was made in July 1977 at the Kansas City Ecumenical Conference entitled *Unity in the Lordship of Jesus*. Quoted from David Cloud's *A Timeline of 20th Century Apostasy* on his website: http://www.wayoflife.org.

[52] Robert Runcie (1921-2000) was the Archbishop of Canterbury from 1980 to 1991.

[53] The Baptist World Alliance is a fellowship of some Baptist unions and conventions around the world.

[54] Dave Hunt *A Woman Rides the Beast; The Catholic Church in the Last Days* (Harvest House Publishers, 1994, p.424).

[55] D. Martyn Lloyd-Jones *Sound an Alarm* (Oct 29, 1969). This address was delivered at the BEC conference at Westminster Chapel. Printed in *Unity in Truth* (Evangelical Press, 1991, edited by H. Rees Jones, p.76).

[56] Dr. Edward Panosian is a retired professor of history and of church history at Bob Jones University.

[57] Quoted by David Cloud *The World Council of Churches* (Way of Life Literature, 2001, p.4).

[58] Please refer to *The Constitution of the British Evangelical Council* (1969 and reprinted in 1998) for the exact wording.

[59] British Evangelical Council *Official Statement: Attitude to Ecumenicity* (BEC Newsletter, June, 1968).

[60] Ibid.

[61] The Evangelical Alliance, formed in 1846, is an organisation of evangelical denominations, churches, organisations and individual Christians.

[62] D. Martyn Lloyd-Jones *The Sword and the Song* (9th Nov, 1977). This was a BEC address. Printed in *Unity in Truth* (Evangelical Press, 1991, edited by Hywel Rees Jones, p.167).

[63] D. Martyn Lloyd-Jones *Consider Your Ways: The Outline of a New Strategy*. This was an address given to the members of the Westminster Fellowship of Ministers on the occasion of their annual outing to Welwyn on 19th June, 1963. Printed in *Knowing the Times: Addresses Delivered on Various Occasions 1942-1977.* (The Banner of Truth Trust, 1989, p.195).

[64] Reg Burrows *Dare to Contend! A Call to Anglican Evangelicals* (Jude Publications, 1990, p.61). The Bible verse in this quotation is from the New International Version (NIV).

[65] David P. Kingdon *The Biblical Attitude to Erroneous Teaching* (British Evangelical Council, 1966).

[66] D. Martyn Lloyd-Jones *Luther and his message for today* (1 Nov, 1967). This was a BEC address and the verbatim quotation is taken from the recorded message.

[67] D. Martyn Lloyd-Jones' sermon on 1 Cor. 16:13-14 (1st November, 1974). Quoted in J. Brencher's *Martyn Lloyd-Jones (1899-1981) and Twentieth-Century Evangelicalism* (Paternoster Press, 2002, p.129).

[68] Dr. Peter Masters and Rev. David Fountain *Today's FIEC and E. J. Poole-Connor* (Sword and Trowel, 2000, No.2, pp.16-19).

[69] C. H. Spurgeon *The Sword and the Trowel*, Nov 1887. Printed in *The 'Down Grade' Controversy* (Pilgrim Publications, 1978, p.35).

[70] British Evangelical Council *Official Statement: Attitude to Ecumenicity* (BEC Newsletter, June, 1968).

[71] Ibid.

[72] Ibid.

[73] Ibid.

[74] Ibid.

[75] See 'BEC's vision' at http://www.grace.org.uk/churches/bec/vision

[76] British Evangelical Council *Official Statement: Attitude to Ecumenicity* (BEC Newsletter, June, 1968).

[77] Ibid.

[78] *BEC Newsletter* (No. 32, Spring 1984).

[79] Rev. T. O. Jenkins (1915-2003) was the British Home Director of the European Missionary Fellowship (EMF) from 1952-1985.

[80] Rev. T. O. Jenkins *Drifting*. Printed in *Vision of Europe* (EMF, July-September, 1984, p.6).

[81] Ibid.

[82] Ibid.

[83] Jonathan Stephen became the Director of the new 'Affinity' in 2003 and continued in this post until 2009.

[84] Jonathan Stephen speaking at the launch of Affinity as reported in the article entitled *To Affinity and beyond* by John Benton in *Evangelicals Now* (May, 2004).

[85] Rev. Roger Fay is the pastor of Zion Evangelical Church in Ripon and the editor of the *Evangelical Times*.

[86] Rev. Roger Fay reporting on the launch of Affinity in *Evangelical Times* (May, 2004).

[87] Rev. John Thackway is the pastor of Holywell Evangelical Church and the editor of the *Bible League Quarterly*.

[88] Rev. John Thackway *Affinity* (Bible League Quarterly, April /June, 2005). Please see: http://www.bibleleaguetrust.org/articles/affinity.pdf

[89] *Affinity* (Issue 6, 2006. No.2).

[90] Michael C. Buss *Who's being divisive? Some thoughts on what the B.E.C. is all about with especial reference to the proposed 'local' councils of evangelical churches.* (British Evangelical Council, 1970, p.8)

[91] The Yorkshire Gospel Partnership consists of a number of Christian churches and organisations in Yorkshire. The Midlands Gospel Partnership consists of Christian churches in the specified area.

[92] D. Martyn Lloyd-Jones *True and False Religion* (17 Oct, 1973). This address was delivered at the BEC annual conference at Westminster Chapel. Printed in *Unity in Truth* (Evangelical Press, 1991, edited by H. Rees Jones, p.157).

[93] D. Martyn Lloyd-Jones *The Sword and the Song* (9 Oct, 1977). This BEC address is printed in *Unity in Truth* (Evangelical Press, 1991, edited by H. Rees Jones, p.178).

[94] The Church of St Barnabas and St Jude, Sandyford, Newcastle upon Tyne.

[95] The BEC newsletter *In Step* (No. 48, Spring 1992).

[96] Rev. Reg Burrows wrote the book *Dare to Contend* (Jude Publications, 1990) in which he pleaded with Anglican evangelicals to take action against the apostasy in the Church of England.

[97] Rev. Vernon Higham was the minister of Heath Evangelical Church in Cardiff from 1962-2002.

[98] Conversation with Rev. Vernon Higham at his home on 28th May, 2007. On 11th January 2012 permission was kindly given to print this statement.

[99] C. H. Spurgeon *Notes,* Oct 1888 (*The 'Down Grade' Controversy*, Pilgrim Publications, 1978, p.66).

[100] C. H. Spurgeon *The Sword and the Trowel*, Dec 1888. (Printed in the The 'Down Grade' Controversy, Pilgrim Publications, 1978, p.69).

[101] The 'Affinity' website: http://www.affinity.org.uk/ The information written regarding this site is correct at the time of the printing of this booklet in May, 2012.

[102] Rev. Nigel Lacey (1942-2007) was the pastor of Stonham Baptist Church, Bethesda Baptist Church in Stowmarket, Lusaka Baptist Church in Zambia, Africa, and Hope Baptist Chapel in East Ham.

[103] Nigel Lacey *Latest Moves in Evangelical Unity* (2006, p.11).

[104] Ibid, p.13.

[105] J. Elwyn Davies (1925 – 2007) was the Chairman of the BEC (1969-72). He was also one of the chief founders of the Evangelical Movement of Wales (EMW), leading the work as its General Secretary from 1955 to 1990.

[106] J. Elwyn Davies *The Evangelical Movement of Wales* (BEC Newsletter, No. 3, July 1969).

[107] Ibid.

[108] *BEC Newsletter* (No. 30, Spring 1983).

[109] See David Cloud's *New Evangelicalism: Its History, Characteristics and Fruit* (Way of Life Literature, 2006, pp. 96-100) for further details of this characteristic of New Evangelicalism.

[110] The Fellowship of Independent Evangelical Churches (FIEC) was formed in 1922 under the name *A Fellowship of Undenominational and Unattached Churches and Missions*. Former leaders include Rev. E. J. Poole-Connor and Rev. T. H. Bendor-Samuel.

[111] D. Martyn Lloyd-Jones *The Call to Liberty* (1972). This is a transcript of the recording of this address given at the FIEC Annual Assembly.

[112] Ibid.

[113] D. Martyn Lloyd-Jones *Evangelical Unity: An Appeal* (18-19 Oct, 1966). Address given at the Second National Assembly of Evangelicals. Published in *Knowing the Times* (The Banner of Truth Trust, 1989, p.252).

[114] D. Martyn Lloyd-Jones *Luther and his message for today* (1 Nov, 1967). Printed in *Unity in Truth* (Evangelical Press, 1991, edited by H. Rees Jones, p.43).

[115] D. Martyn Lloyd-Jones *The Mayflower Pilgrims* (1 Oct,1970). This was a BEC address delivered at Westminster Chapel. Printed in *Unity in Truth* (Evangelical Press, 1991, edited by H. Rees Jones, p.100).

[116] T. H. Bendor-Samuel *New Delhi and After: An Examination of Developments in the Ecumenical Movement* (British Evangelical Council, 1963, pp.12-13). The title of this booklet relates to the third great Assembly of the WCC at New Delhi late in 1961.

[117] D. Martyn Lloyd-Jones *Evangelical Unity: An Appeal* (18-19 Oct, 1966). Address given at the Second National Assembly of Evangelicals. Published in *Knowing the Times* (The Banner of Truth Trust, 1989, p.256).

[118] British Evangelical Council *Official Statement: Attitude to Ecumenicity* (BEC Newsletter, June, 1968).

[119] Telephone conversation with Rev. Paul Bassett on 18th May, 2012. Printed with kind permission.

[120] John Gwyn-Thomas (1923-1977) was vicar of St Paul's, Cambridge and a Biblical expositor.

[121] Philip Edgcumbe Hughes (1915-1990) was an Anglican clergyman and scholar.

[122] Telephone conversation with Dr. Christopher Catherwood on June 11th, 2007. Permission was kindly given to print this statement at that time and was confirmed in a conversation on January 7th, 2012.

[123] Rev. Harry Waite was the minister of Thornton Heath Evangelical Church from 1959 to 1993.

[124] The Westminster Fellowship began in 1941 as a meeting at Westminster Chapel for pastors and men in positions of Christian leadership. It was led by Dr. Lloyd-Jones.

[125] Rev. Robert Sheehan, a member of the Westminster Fellowship in Dr. Lloyd-Jones' time said of him: 'He was certainly willing to preach for men in mixed denominations. His policy could be summarised in the phrases "brotherliness without approval" or "limited fellowship" (*C. H. Spurgeon and the Modern Church*, Grace Publications, 1985, p.111).

[126] Telephone conversation with Rev. Harry Waite on 7th January, 2012. Printed with kind permission.

[127] Dr. Martyn Lloyd-Jones speaking at the Westminster Fellowship, July 3rd, 1967.

[128] C. H. Spurgeon's sermon (no. 2047) *No Compromise*, preached at the Metropolitan Tabernacle, Newington on Oct 7th, 1888.

[129] Rev. T. O. Jenkins was part of a group of men from the Westminster Fellowship who, in 1983, called for a return to the stand made by Dr. Lloyd-Jones against ecumenism. See R.J. Sheehan's *C. H. Spurgeon and the Modern Church* (Grace Publications Trust, 1985, p.115 and footnote number 45, p.124).

[130] 'A secondary separatist would be one who will not cooperate with (1) apostates; or (2) evangelical believers who aid and abet the apostates by their continued organisational or cooperative alignment with them' (Ernest Pickering *Biblical Separation*. Printed by Regular Baptist Press, 1979, p.217). Some secondary separatists go further than this and separate from those who fellowship with those in the second category.

[131] Rev. T. O. Jenkins *Drifting* (Vision of Europe, July-September, 1984, p.6).

[132] Ibid.

[133] Ibid.

[134] Ibid.

[135] Jenkins, T. O. *Letter to the Editor* ('Fellowship' Magazine, May/June, 1984).

[136] Robert Sheehan *C. H. Spurgeon and the Modern Church* (Grace Publications Trust, 1985, p.115).

[137] Ibid., p.113.

[138] Peter Masters *Stand for the Truth* (formerly *Separation and Obedience*) (Sword & Trowel, 1983).

[139] Iain H. Murray *D. Martyn Lloyd-Jones: The Fight of Faith: 1939-1981* (The Banner of Truth Trust, 1990, pp.536-7).

[140] Conversation with Rev. Graham Harrison at his home on June 25th 2007. Printed with kind permission.

[141] Robert Sheehan *C. H. Spurgeon and the Modern Church* (Grace Publications Trust, 1985, p.111).

[142] British Evangelical Council *Official Statement: Attitude to Ecumenicity* (BEC Newsletter, June, 1968).

[143] Ibid.

[144] D. Martyn Lloyd-Jones *A Policy Appropriate to Biblical Faith* (1st Oct, 1954). This address was given at the Annual Meeting of the Inter-Varsity Fellowship of Students in London. The notes were taken by Dr. Douglas Johnson. Published in *Knowing the Times* (The Banner of Truth Trust, 1989, p.59).

[145] T. H. Bendor-Samuel *New Delhi and After: An Examination of Developments in the Ecumenical Movement* (British Evangelical Council, 1963, pp.3-4).

Comments

'I was converted in 1964 and so I have lived through the era covered by this thrilling article. I have no hesitation in congratulating Ruth for bringing back into focus those issues for which many of us stood and still stand. Every believer should read the article prayerfully, but with this warning that once you begin to read, you will not stop until you come to the end.'
Rev. Teify Ebenezer (Pastor of Zion Baptist Church, Brynmawr, S. Wales)

'This little gem of a book can be read within half an hour, but its subject matter is weighty and demands much pondering. It is a tribute to those who stood for Gospel purity against the pressure of ecumenical compromise in the latter part of the Twentieth Century. It is also a timely reminder of the issues which are still very much at stake, and a warning against a careless and negligent drift into the same errors today. I believe this book can do much good and ought to be in the hands of every church member.'
Rev. Roland Burrows (Pastor of Ebenezer Baptist Chapel, Cradley Heath, Birmingham)

'We are thankful to God that Miss Palgrave has gathered together this band of faithful witnesses proving the dangerous drift that has occurred among evangelicals over the last 50 years. It is our prayer that this vital warning will bring about repentance among the 21st Century evangelicals who have determined to sideline their wise and careful "fathers" in the Gospel.'
Rev. Peter Ratcliff (Minister of St Johns, Merton Abbey Mills, Church of England Continuing and Editor of *The English Churchman*)

'My former independent church was transferred from BEC to Affinity without any consultation. We immediately cancelled our membership for the reasons outlined in this booklet. All who have a concern to maintain the truth of the Gospel without compromise should read this booklet. I warmly commend it.'
Alec Taylor (Retired pastor of Chelmsley Wood Reformed Baptist Church, Birmingham)

'An enduring testimony lives on – well-researched evidence that clearly shows that modern day evangelicalism has to a large extent drifted from its Biblical moorings.'
Rev. Neil Pfeiffer (Pastor of Peniel Green Congregational Church, Swansea)